1, 2, & 3 JOHN

1, 2, & 3 JOHN

VERSE-BY-VERSE GRAPHIC NOVEL WEB TRANSLATION

ILLUSTRATIONS BY THOMAS FASANO

1, 2, & 3 JOHN: VERSE-BY-VERSE GRAPHIC NOVEL WEB TRANSLATION

Illustrations Copyright © 2025 by Thomas Fasano

The World English Bible is in the public domain.

Published by Coyote Canyon Press
Claremont, California

ISBN: 979-8-9937072-0-4

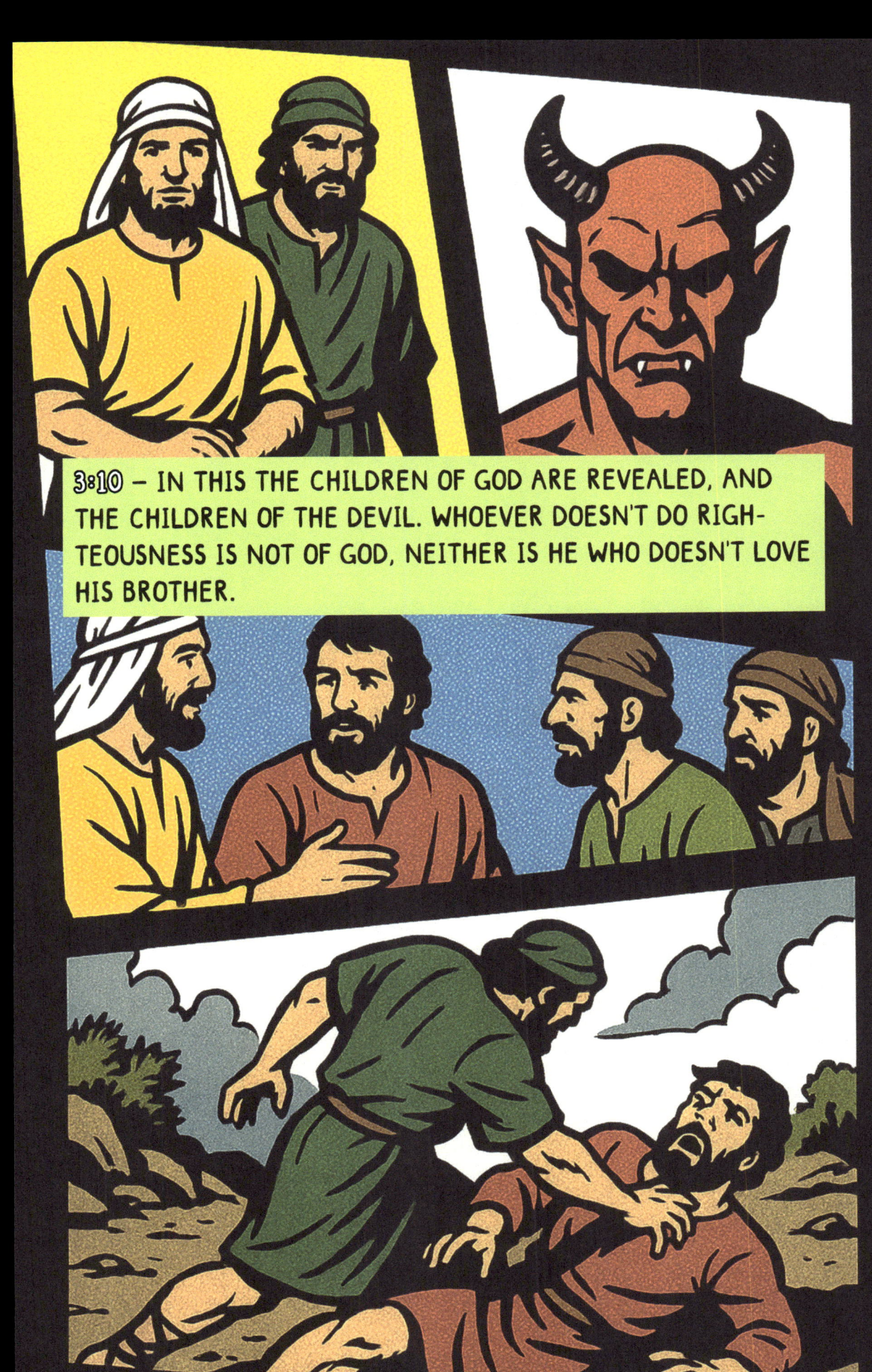

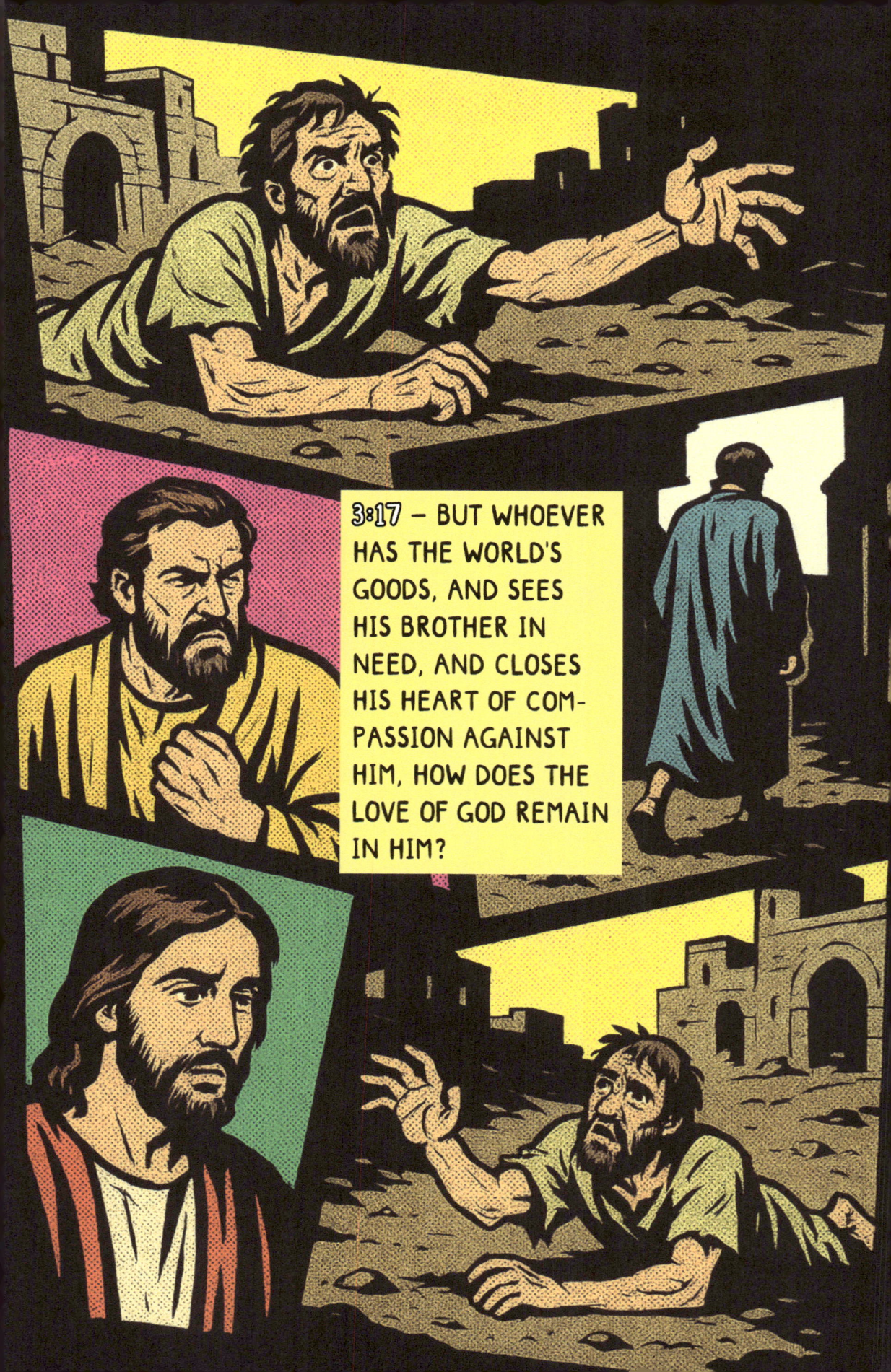

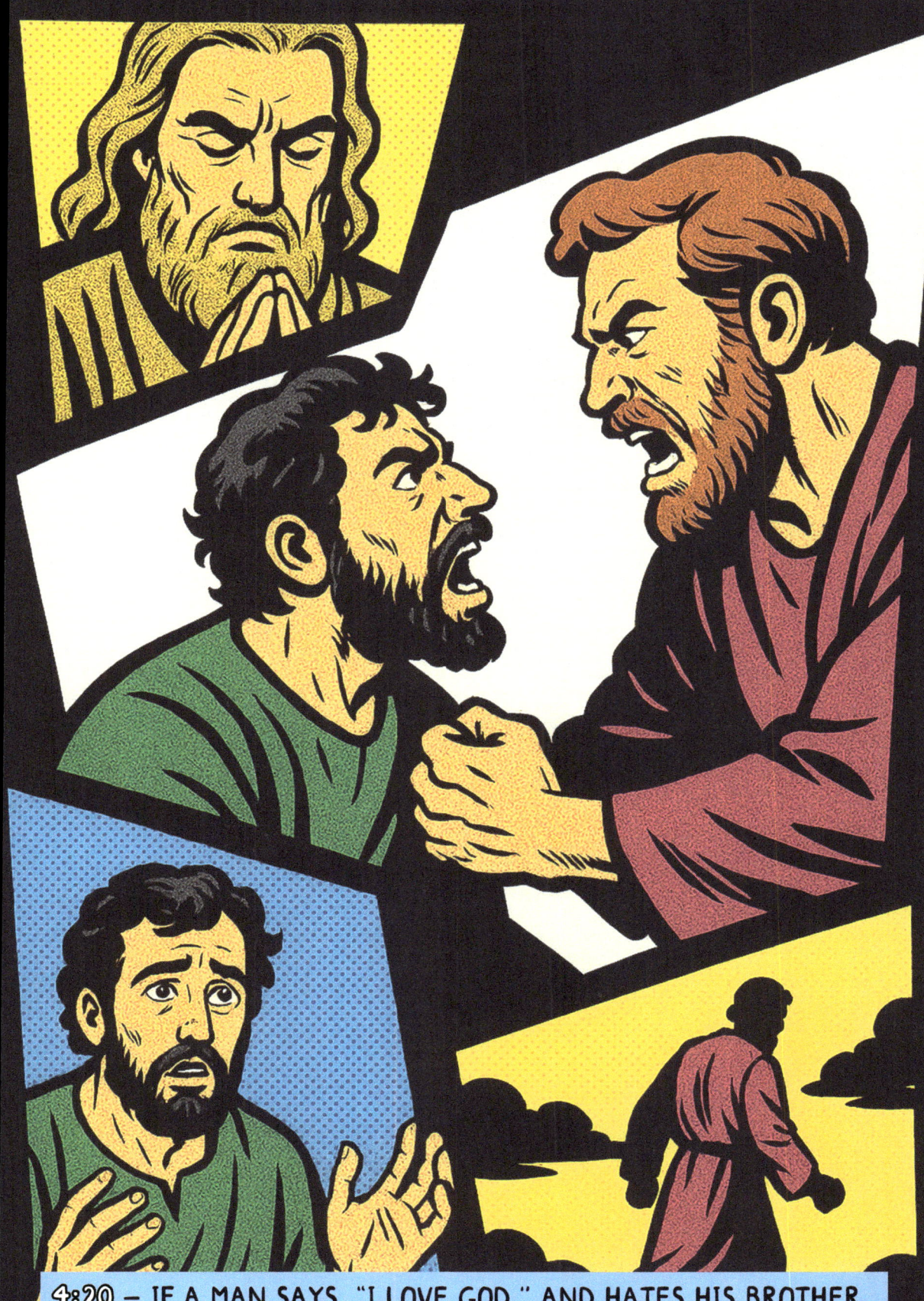

5:20 – WE KNOW THAT THE SON OF GOD HAS COME, AND HAS GIVEN US AN UNDERSTANDING, THAT WE KNOW HIM WHO IS TRUE, AND WE ARE IN HIM WHO IS TRUE, IN HIS SON JESUS CHRIST. THIS IS THE TRUE GOD, AND ETERNAL LIFE.

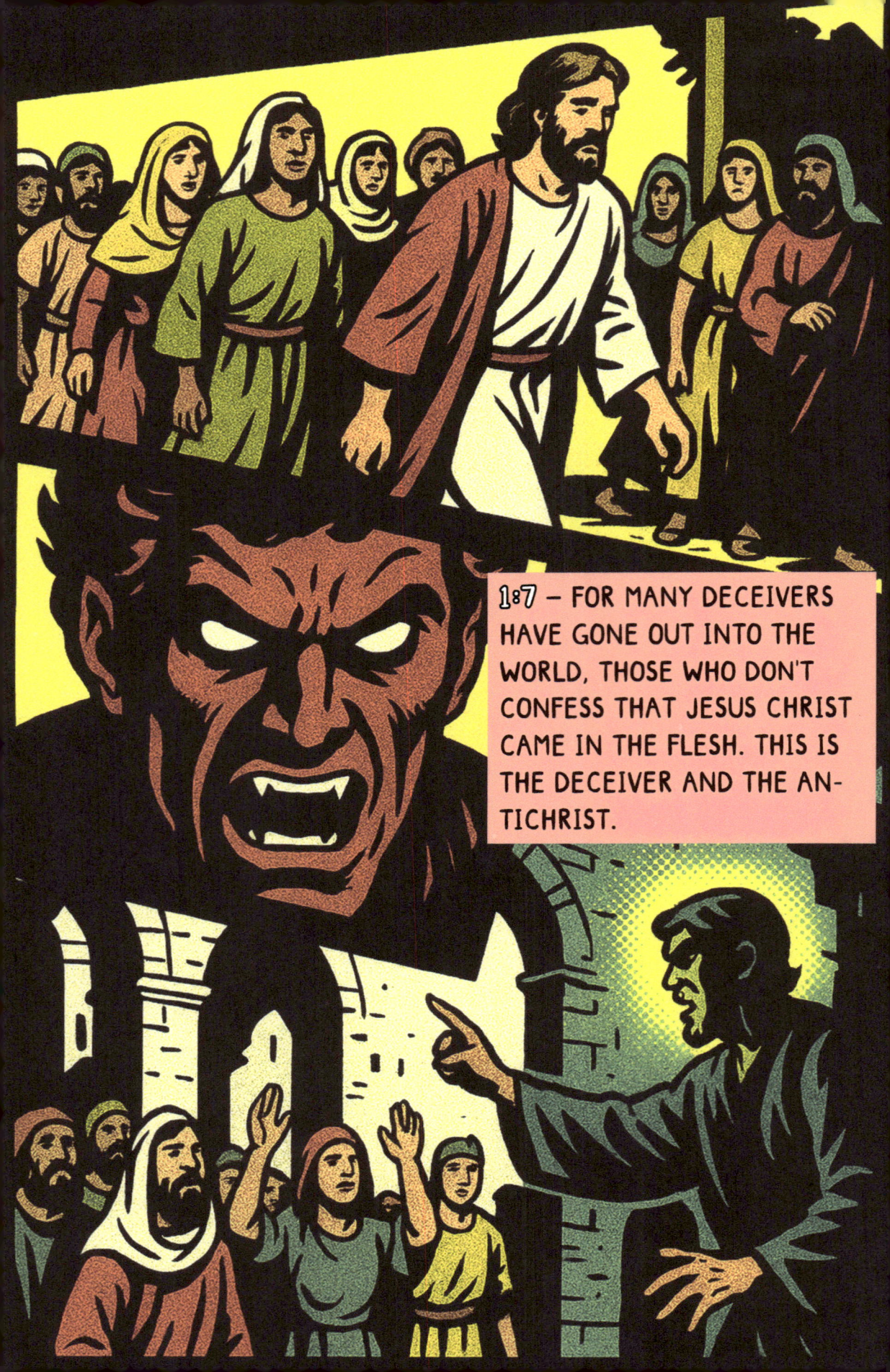

1:10 – IF ANYONE COMES TO YOU, AND DOESN'T BRING THIS TEACHING, DON'T RECEIVE HIM INTO YOUR HOUSE, AND DON'T WELCOME HIM,

www.ingramcontent.com/pod-product-compliance
Lightning Source LLC
Chambersburg PA
CBHW061115170426
43198CB00026B/2990